Yorkshire Terrier

Charles and Linda George

Created by Q2AMedia
www.q2amedia.com
Editor Jeff O' Hare
Publishing Director Chester Fisher
Client Service Manager Santosh Vasudevan
Project Manager Kunal Mehrotra
Art Director Harleen Mehta
Designer Cheena yadav
Picture Researcher Nivisha Sinha

Library of Congress Cataloging-in-Publication Data
George, Charles, 1949-
Yorkshire terrier / [Charles George, Linda George].
p. cm. — (Top dogs)
Includes index.
ISBN 0-531-24936-0/978-0-531-24936-9/ (pbk.)
1. Yorkshire terrier—Juvenile literature. I. George, Linda. II. Title.
SF429.Y6G46 2010
636.76—dc22
2010035038

This edition published by Scholastic Inc.,

Printed and bound in Heshan, China
232755 10/10
10 9 8 7 6 5 4 3 2 1

Picture Credits
t= top, b= bottom, c= center, r= right, l= left

Cover Page: Juniors Bildarchiv/Photolibrary.

Title Page: Konstantin Gushcha/Shutterstock.

4-5: Pixshots/Shutterstock; 6: Nata Sdobnikova/Shutterstock; 6-7: Jonathan Hill/
Istockphoto; 8: Cherry Hills/Photolibrary; 8-9: Caroline Brinkmann/Photolibrary; 10-11:
Juniors Bildarchiv/Photolibrary; 11: Pavel Timofeyev/Istockphoto; 12-13: Donna Coleman/
Istockphoto; 14: Krzyssagit/Dreamstime; 14-15: Caroline Brinkmann/Photolibrary, Halp/
Shutterstock; 16: Objectif MC/Shutterstock; 17: Pavel Timofeyev/Istockphoto; 18: Caroline
Brinkmann/Photolibrary; 18-19: Argo/Shutterstock; 20: Felix Mizioznikov/Shutterstock; 21:
Ericsphotography/Istockphoto; 22-23: Gunter Flegar/Photolibrary; 23: Joy Brown/Shutterstock;
24-25: Mark Herreid/Shutterstock; 26-27: Katherine Moffitt/Istockphoto; 28-29: Libby Welsh/
Janine Wiedel Photolibrary/Alamy; 30: Wm. A. Wynne; 31: Wm. A. Wynne.

Q2AMedia Art Bank: 5.

Contents

What are Yorkshire Terriers?

People in the U.S. love Yorkshire terriers. Most people call them Yorkies. Yorkies are small dogs that think they are big dogs! They bark at anything new. They even bark at much bigger dogs!

Yorkshire terriers got their name from Yorkshire, England. When they came to the U.S., they were called Yorkies. A long time ago, Yorkies were trained to be "ratters." They chased and killed rats.

Fast Fact

Yorkies came to the U.S. from England and Scotland.

Everyone Loves Yorkies!

Fast Fact

It may be hard to teach a Yorkie to get along with a cat!

A Yorkie loves its home. It acts like it owns the house. It barks at dogs, cats, and people it doesn't know. A Yorkie must be taught how to get along with other animals.

Fast Fact

Your Yorkie will love you as the most special person in its life!

Yorkies curl up in your lap to take a nap. They like to sleep on your bed. They may sleep right next to your face! They may sleep behind the pillows on the couch.

A Yorkie puppy is tiny. When it is born, it weighs 3-4 ounces (85-113 gm). That's about as much as a deck of cards. A **newborn** teacup Yorkie is even smaller!

Fast Fact

A newborn Yorkie puppy may fit in the palm of your hand.

The smallest Yorkie that ever lived was named Big Boss. Fully grown, Big Boss was about the size of a softball. He was only 4.7 inches (11.9 cm) tall and 5.1 inches (13 cm) long!

Fast Fact

The owner of a Yorkie may have the puppy's tail **docked** when it is very young.

Big Little Dogs!

A long time ago, Yorkies were bigger dogs. They weighed between 12 and 14 pounds (5.4-6.4 kg). In time, people wanted smaller Yorkies. Today, Yorkies weigh around 7 pounds (3.2 kg). They stand 8-9 inches tall (20.3-22.9 cm).

Fast Fact

A Yorkie can sometimes get hurt by bigger dogs. It is too brave to know when it should run away.

Yorkies act like bigger dogs. Yorkies protect their owners from people and animals. They may bite if a stranger gets too close.

Yorkies and Kids

A Yorkie is a sturdy little dog, but it should be handled gently. A Yorkie likes to play, but sometimes, very young children can play too rough. An adult should watch to make sure the Yorkie doesn't get hurt.

Fast Fact

Yorkies are smart dogs. They can also be **stubborn**!

A Yorkie likes lots of attention. Your Yorkie can get upset if you don't spend time with it. Train your Yorkie to behave when it's little. Then, it will know how to be sweet when it grows up.

Fast Fact

Yorkies will bite if they think you will harm them. Be careful.

Choosing a Yorkie Puppy

Choose a healthy puppy. Your puppy should be ready to play. A male Yorkie moves around more than a female. Choose a puppy that fits your family. An active family should choose an active puppy.

Fast Fact

A **litter** of Yorkies usually has 4 or 5 puppies.

A Yorkie is black and tan when it's born. As it grows older, its hair turns grayish-blue. A Yorkie's hair grows long and silky. Show dogs must keep their hair long. Other Yorkies may have shorter hair.

Fast Fact

Yorkies get lots of exercise playing inside. They also like going on short walks.

Taking Care of Your Yorkie Puppy

A Yorkie's hair needs to be brushed every day. You can take your Yorkie to a dog **groomer**. A groomer will bathe and brush your Yorkie. A Yorkie loves being groomed.

Yorkie pups need food made just for puppies. Don't give table food to your puppies. Stick to puppy treats. Yorkies have tender tummies. They also need plenty of cool water to drink.

Fast Fact

Never give a dog chocolate or raisins. These foods can make a dog very sick.

Brushing Hair and Clipping Nails

A Yorkie has beautiful hair. It can grow long and silky. It can get tangled, so it has to be brushed often. Brushing keeps a Yorkie's hair soft.

Fast Fact

A groomer can trim your dog's nails and put nail polish on them.

Yorkies can have their hair clipped. No more tangles! When their hair is short, it curls. This makes them nice to pet. Yorkies do not **shed** their hair. They are good dogs for people who are allergic to dog hair.

Fast Fact

A Yorkie usually wears a red bow in its hair for a dog show.

Busy Yorkies

Fast Fact

Keep your Yorkie on a leash when you are outside. This helps you keep it out of harm's way.

Yorkies have lots of energy. They love to play "Fetch!" Sometimes, they don't bring back the ball. They want you to come and get it! Yorkies also love going for walks. They like to smell other animals that have passed by.

Walk your Yorkie with a **harness**. If you use a collar, your Yorkie might choke. It can pull too hard on the **leash**. Give your Yorkie time to explore. Your dog thinks it is the "top dog" where you live!

Fast Fact

A Yorkie likes toys that make noises when it plays with them.

Pampered Pups

Fast Fact

Yorkies do well in small houses or apartments.

A Yorkie doesn't need much room. If you have a fenced back yard, your Yorkie will probably have plenty of room to run. If not, you'll need to take it for a short walk each day so it can get some exercise.

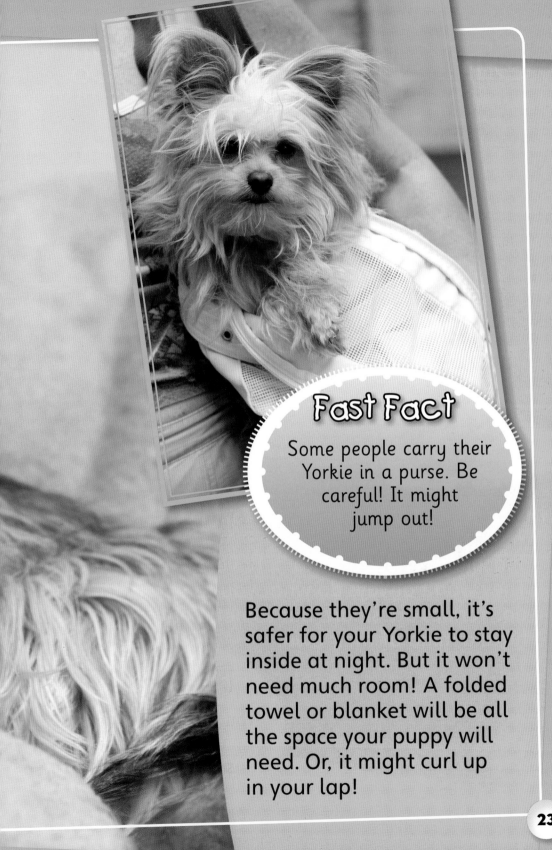

Fast Fact

Some people carry their Yorkie in a purse. Be careful! It might jump out!

Because they're small, it's safer for your Yorkie to stay inside at night. But it won't need much room! A folded towel or blanket will be all the space your puppy will need. Or, it might curl up in your lap!

Smart Yorkies!

Teaching Yorkies how to behave can be hard. They won't always do what you tell them to do. Yorkies are smart, but sometimes can have a mind of their own.

Fast Fact

You will have to teach your Yorkie the same lesson over and over.

Be **patient** with your Yorkie. Choose a quiet place for **training**. When your Yorkie gets tired, let it do something else. It may want to take a nap. Learning can be hard work!

Fast Fact

When you leave your Yorkie, let it sleep on one of your shirts. Your smell will keep your Yorkie from being too lonely.

A Yorkie will choose one person to love the most. Yorkies make good **companion dogs**. Be gentle to your Yorkie.

Yorkies are friendly dogs. They are faithful and loving. They may feel sad when you have to leave for a while. Be sure to leave toys for your Yorkies to play with.

Fast Fact

Your Yorkie may cry when you go out. It will be glad to see you when you come back!

Yorkies Helping People

A guide dog helps people who can't see. A service dog helps people who can't hear or walk. A Yorkie is too small to help someone who can't walk. It can help a person who can't hear.

Fast Fact

A Yorkie can be trained to jump if the phone rings. It can also tell its owner when someone is at the door.

Yorkies are friendly dogs. Their owners can take them to visit people who are sick or who live alone. Yorkies help these people feel better. The dogs love to be petted and held.

Fast Fact

Most people like to hold and pet a cute little Yorkie.

Fast Fact

Smoky won awards for being so brave.

Smoky was a **female** Yorkie owned by a **soldier**. Smoky was very brave. She saved her owner's life. She barked when she heard enemy soldiers coming.

SMOKY

Once, Smoky's owner told her to crawl through a long dark pipe under the ground. Smoky didn't want to, but she did. She pulled a telephone wire through the pipe. Her actions helped save the soldiers **positioned** near her.

Glossary

Allergic – having a medical condition in which a person sneezes or otherwise reacts to something he or she comes into contact with

Companion dogs – pets; dogs trained to be friends with people

Docked – cut a dog's tail to keep it short

Groomer – a person who earns money by cutting dogs' hair and trimming their nails

Harness – a web of straps that go around a dog's chest and neck

Leash – a strap attached to a dog's collar or harness and used to help control a dog while on a walk

Litter – a group of puppies born to one mother, all at the same time

Newborn – a dog or other animal that has just been born

Patient – able to wait

Positioned – put in place

Ratter – a dog trained to hunt and kill mice and rats

Shed – lose hair

Soldier – someone fighting for his or her country

Statue – a memorial, usually carved from stone

Stubborn – determined to do things in a certain way

Sturdy – strong; not easily hurt

Training – teaching a skill

Index